I0199355

The Frog's Golden Water

Adam Altman
Author

Caroline Whelan
Illustrator

© Copyright 2018, Adam Altman

All Rights Reserved

No part of this book may be reproduced, stored in a
retrieval system, or transmitted by any means, electronic,
mechanical, photocopying, recording, or otherwise,
without written permission from the author.

ISBN: 978-1-64204-212-2

This Book Belongs to

_____.

The sun was very bright, and
Skippy, the frog, was swimming in his
favorite pond. The water was golden
because of the reflection from the sun.
The sun always managed to shine on the pond
even when the clouds covered most of the sky.

The frog was waiting for his friends, Chirpie and Snuffie, to come for a visit. The bluebird and the dog were Skippy's best friends.

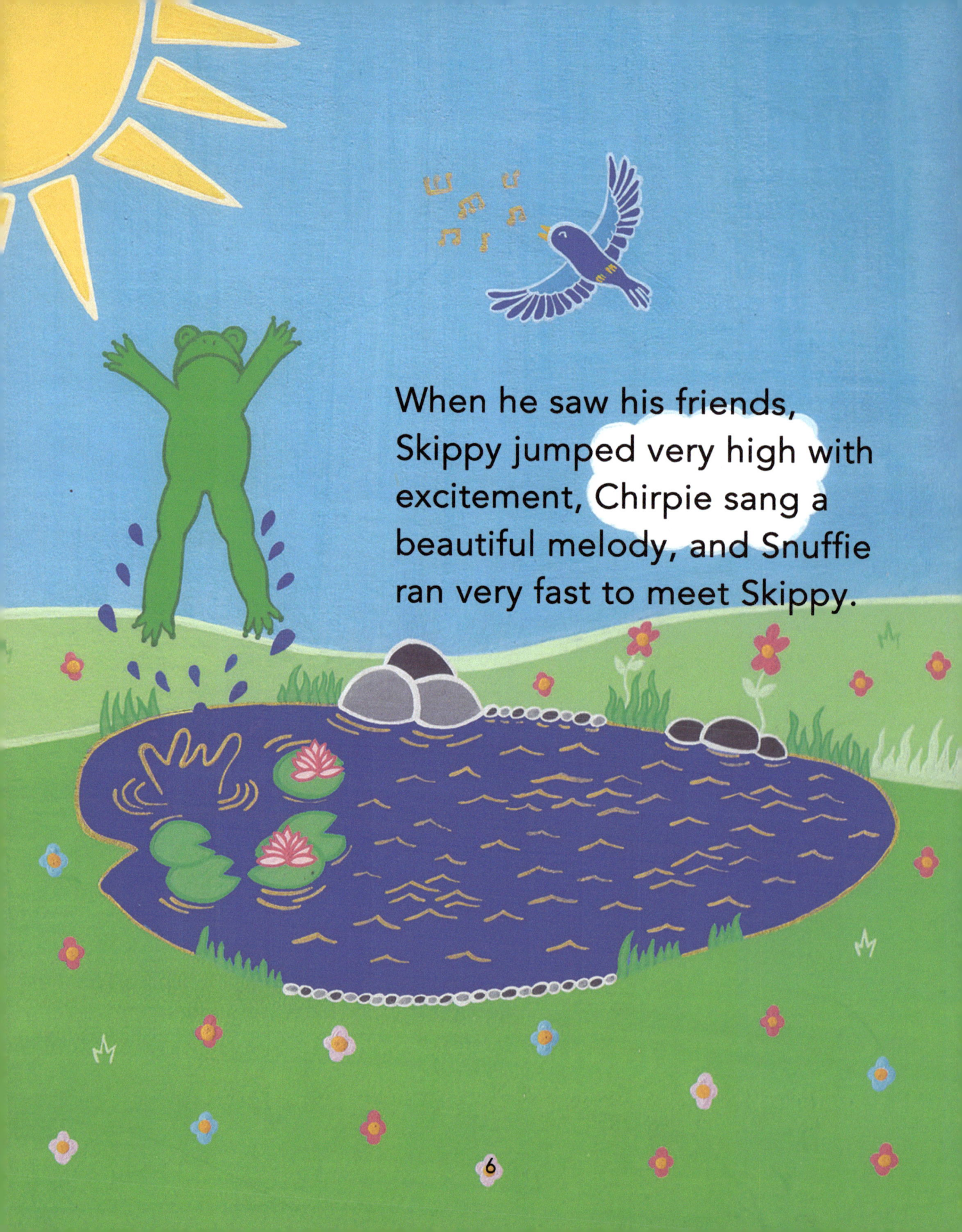

When he saw his friends, Skippy jumped very high with excitement, Chirpie sang a beautiful melody, and Snuffie ran very fast to meet Skippy.

From a shadow in the meadow,
Clevo, the toad, watched them.

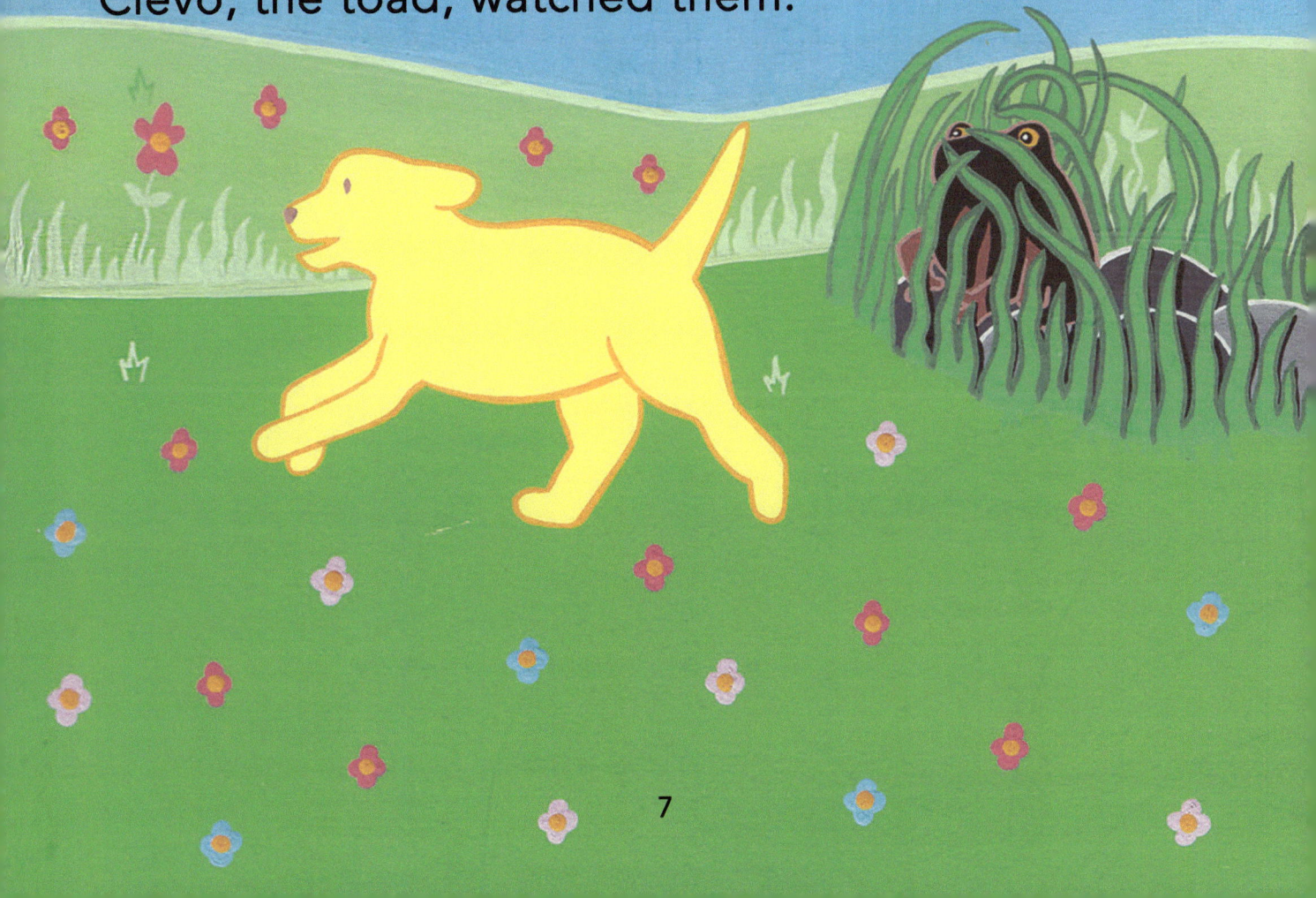

For the whole day, Skippy and his friends played in the meadow or in the pond. Skippy jumped without much control, but that just added to the fun. Since he was still a chick, Chirpie flew clumsily. But his melodies were very sweet. Snuffie played hide and seek very well. She could always find and catch the others with her speed.

Clevo watched the talented animals with envy. The others often asked him to join in on the fun and games, but he never did. One day, Clevo looked sad, so Chirpie tried to cheer him up with a melody. The toad seemed to like the song, but he still did not join the fun.

After Chirpie and Snuffie went home, Skippy went to sleep. It had been another good day.

But that night, something terrible happened.

At dawn, Skippy awoke
and saw Clevo hop away
from the pond. A moment
later, he noticed that
the water was
not golden
anymore.
Worried, Skippy jumped
as high as he could,
unable to control his jumps.
One leap almost caused him to
hit a branch of a tree high above him.

Snuffie saw her friend jumping. She ran as fast as she could to find out why Skippy was leaping so high. She also barked to alarm Chirpie.

"The golden light is gone," cried Skippy when his friends got there.

"Who did this?" barked Snuffie.

"Clevo, that's who," replied Skippy. "I saw him hopping away. He didn't want me to see him."

Then Chirpie sang an inquiring melody as if asking why the toad had done such a thing.

An angry voice came from nearby. "Communicating through a song! I hate that."

Snuffie found Clevo
before he could hop
from his hiding place.
She held the toad with
her paw.

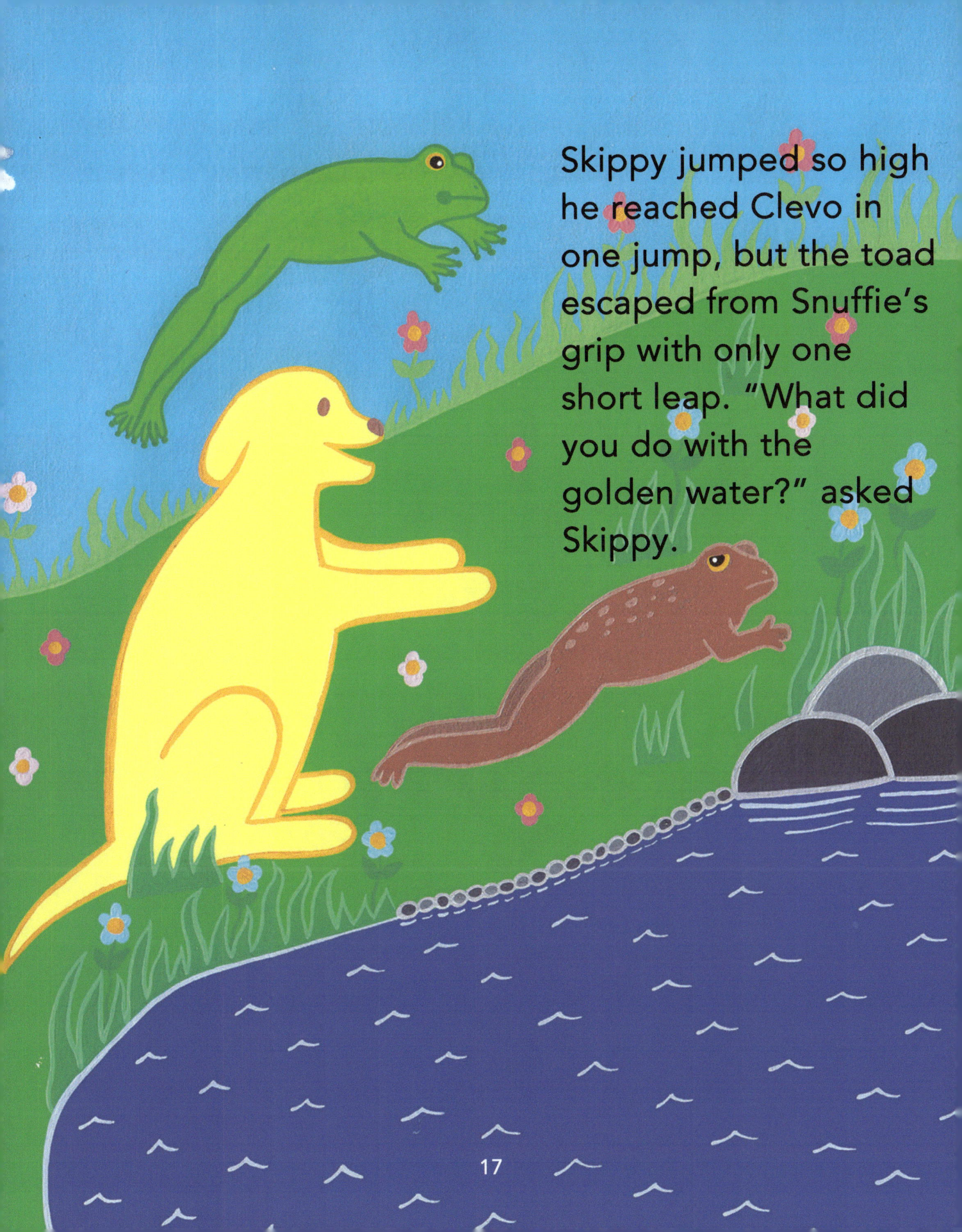

Skippy jumped so high he reached Clevo in one jump, but the toad escaped from Snuffie's grip with only one short leap. "What did you do with the golden water?" asked Skippy.

Clevo was silent for a moment. Then he said, "I didn't do anything, but it serves you right that the light is gone." Then he hopped away.

Skippy sat at the edge of the pond and thought. After a while, he came up with a plan, which Chirpie and Snuffie liked. Thus, they helped Skippy arrange the plan.

It was just a little later that the bear came.
Snuffie ran to find the toad, yelling,
"We need help!"

Clevo came out of
his hiding place.

"Follow me," cried Snuffie.

When they got to the pond, they heard a shriek.
It was Chirpie, trapped in a tree; a bear was clawing
at the bluebird.

Skippy tried to jump above the bear to free Chirpie from the branches that held him.

21

The bear's claws swiped him away. Skippy landed in the pond where the golden light used to be.

"Snuffie, distract the bear," said Clevo.
"I've got an idea."

Snuffie rushed in close, annoying
the bear.

"Grrrrrrr!" growled the bear, stepping towards the dog. Snuffie dashed off.

Although Snuffie had only stopped the bear a moment, Clevo had had enough time to figure out what to do. He made a small jump to the closest branch and then leaped to the next branch. With the ensuing leap, he finally reached Chirpie. Even though Clevo could not jump as high as Skippy, he had still reached Chirpie because of his skillful jumps. He released the branches from the bluebird's wing.

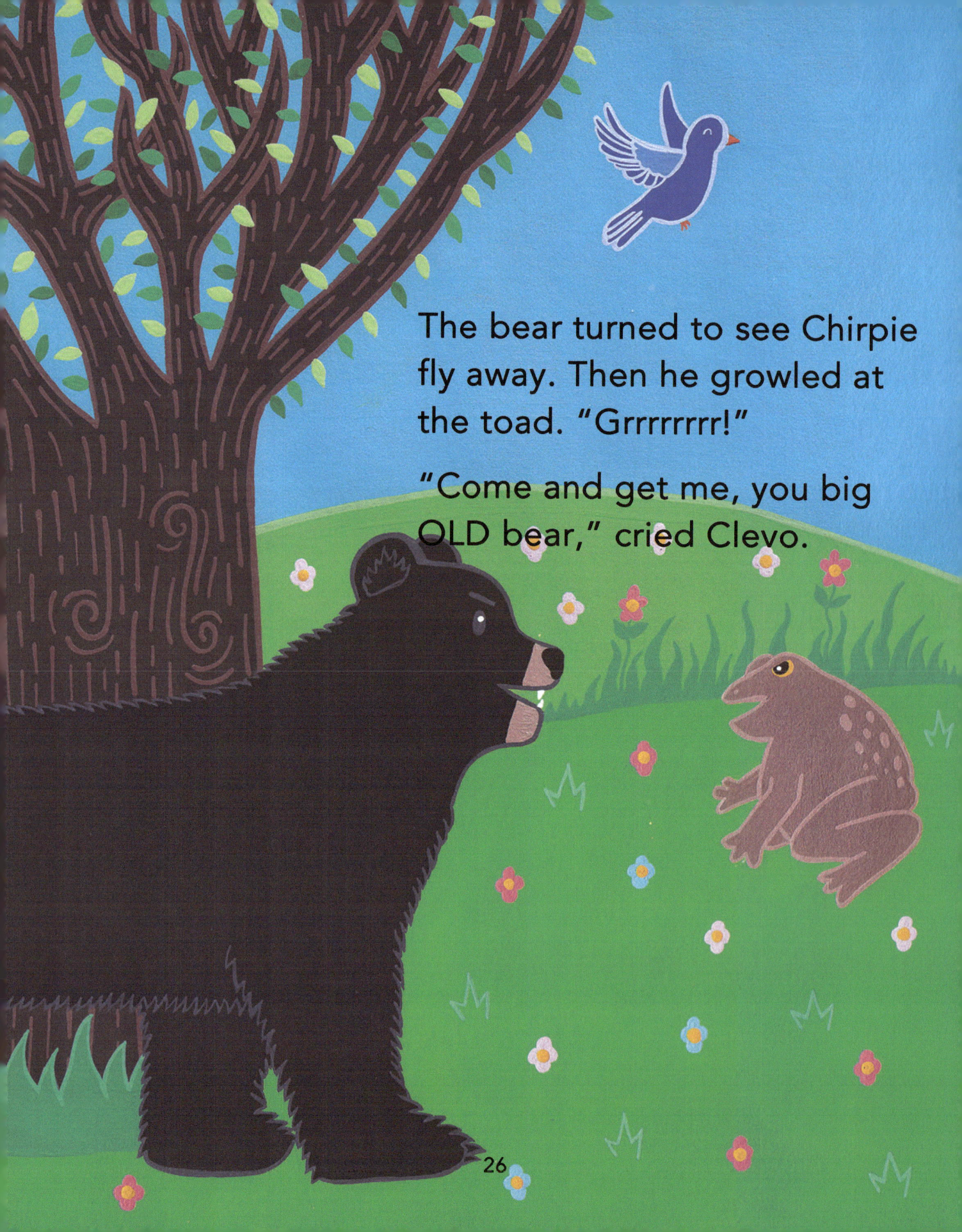

The bear turned to see Chirpie fly away. Then he growled at the toad. "Grrrrrrrr!"

"Come and get me, you big OLD bear," cried Clevo.

As most animals know, bears do not like being called "old". The angry bear chased the toad. Just as the bear was about to catch him, Clevo leaped onto a rock. It moved ever so slightly. In a flash, a ray of the sun's light reflected off the rock and struck the bear in the eyes. The bear was blinded for a moment, allowing enough time for Clevo to escape. After the bear recovered, he gave up the chase and ran away.

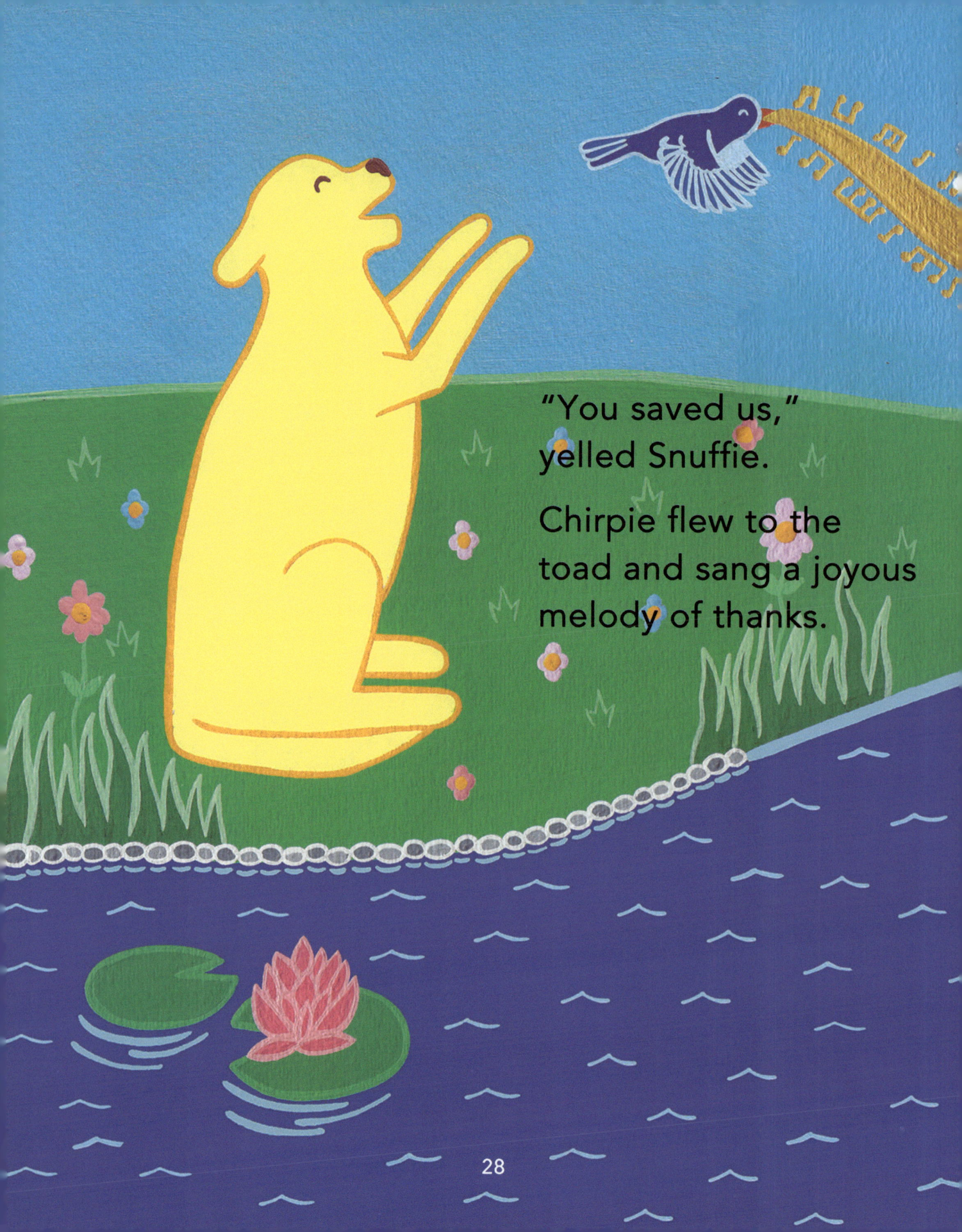

"You saved us," yelled Snuffie.

Chirpie flew to the toad and sang a joyous melody of thanks.

Skippy surfaced from the water to talk to Clevo. "You reflected the sun's light away from the pond, didn't you? That's how it lost its golden color."

The toad looked ashamed. "I'm sorry."

"Well, Clevo, the way you positioned that rock so that it would blind the bear was very clever. You are talented at physics!"

"I am talented," Clevo said as if he had made a discovery.

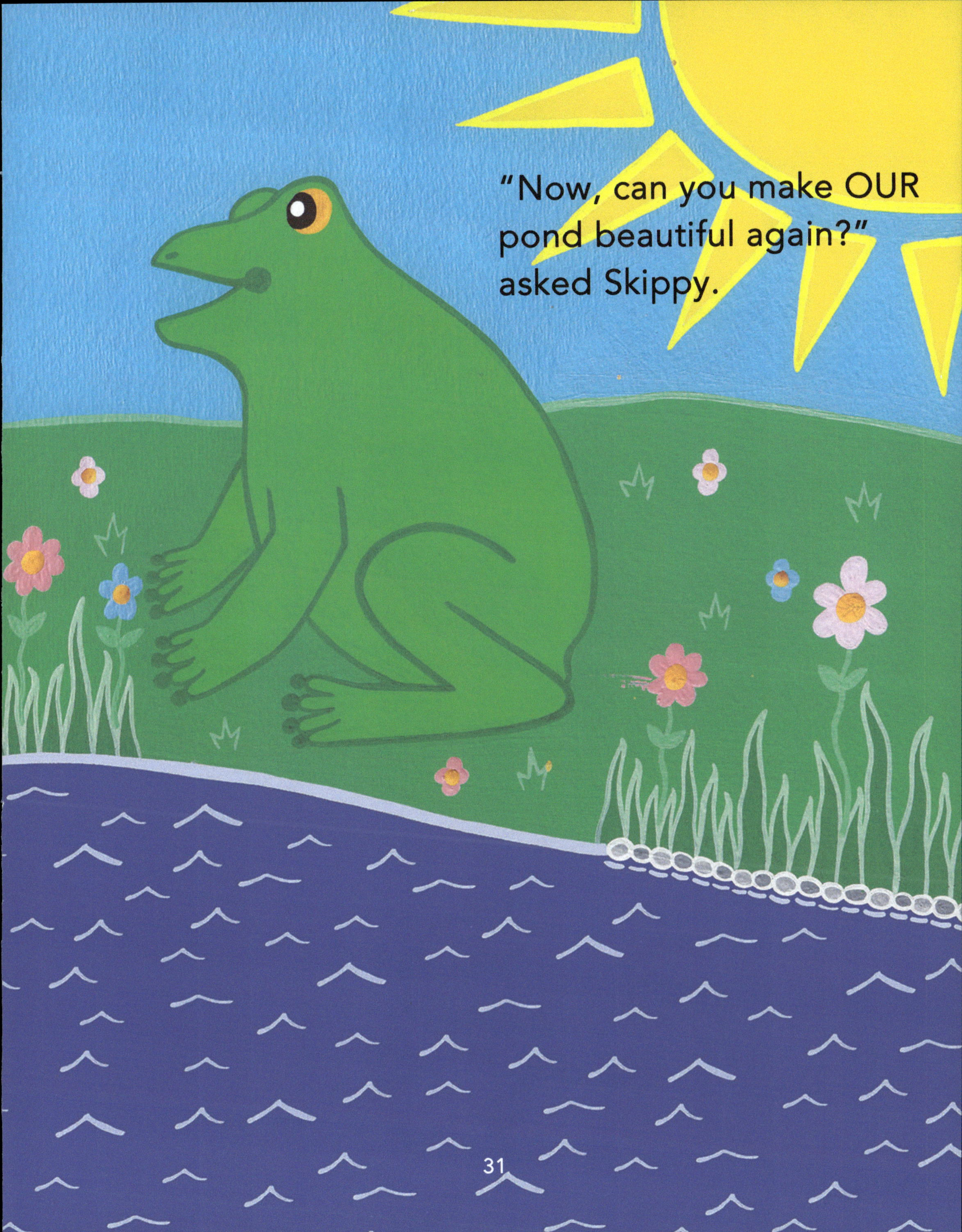

"Now, can you make OUR pond beautiful again?" asked Skippy.

"OUR pond?" the toad responded.

"It's always good to share," said Skippy.

Clevo drew in the dirt to explain where all of the rocks were located and where to move them. Snuffie did what Clevo explained. Then the sun's light reflected spectacularly onto the pond again.

Skippy leaped into the air and carelessly dived into the golden water. Snuffie lapped up some of the water. Chirpie sang happily.

"Maybe you can help me figure out how to jump accurately," Skippy said to the toad after the frog surfaced from the pond.

Clevo agreed to help.
Then he jumped into the golden
pond for the first time.

After the day was
over and Clevo had
departed, Skippy hopped
over to a big tree.
"Thank you, Furry, for your help,"
he said to his friend.

The bear replied, "You're welcome, but I did not like being called 'OLD'!"

Skippy laughed.

The End

Dedicated to my wonderful daughter,
Serriah, who will always be
my sweet little girl.

www.ingramcontent.com/pod-product-compliance
Lightning Source LLC
Chambersburg PA
CBHW042014090426

42811CB00015B/1643

* 9 7 8 1 6 4 2 0 4 2 1 2 2 *